Books in The Tuttle Twins series:

The Tuttle Twins Learn About the Law

The Tuttle Twins and the Miraculous Pencil

The Tuttle Twins and the Creature from Jekyll Island

The Tuttle Twins and the Food Truck Fiasco

The Tuttle Twins and the Road to Surfdom

The Tuttle Twins and the Golden Rule

The Tuttle Twins and the Search for Atlas

The Tuttle Twins and their Spectacular Show Business

The Tuttle Twins and the Fate of the Future

The Tuttle Twins and the Education Vacation

The Tuttle Twins and the Messed Up Market

Find them all at TuttleTwins.com

ISBN 978-1-943521-14-2

Boyack, Connor, author.
Stanfield, Elijah, illustrator.
The Tuttle Twins and the Road to Surfdom / Connor Boyack.

Cover design by Elijah Stanfield
Edited and typeset by Connor Boyack

Printed in the United States

16 15 14 13 12

THE TUTTLE TWINS
and the
ROAD TO Surfdom

PUBLIC TRANSPORTATION PLAN

CONNOR BOYACK

Illustrated by Elijah Stanfield

This book is dedicated to
Charles Koch

for fighting central planning by
freeing the market.

"Are we there yet?" Ethan asked his parents as the Tuttle family sat in bumper-to-bumper traffic on their way to La Playa, their favorite beach.

"We'll be there soon," Mr. Tuttle replied.

"Why are we going this way to the beach, anyway?" Emily wondered out loud. The family's van was stopped in a neighborhood in a long line of cars.

"The road we normally use is blocked off," Mrs. Tuttle explained. "But we're not sure why."

The Tuttles always enjoyed visiting La Playa. The family had many great memories of surfing, snorkeling, and soaking up the warm sun.

Ethan and Emily liked playing at the beach, but they *loved* shopping at La Playa Lane—a boardwalk next to the beach—even more. On each visit to La Playa, they spent many hours playing at the arcade and eating yummy food.

After a drive that took much longer than expected, the Tuttles finally arrived at La Playa and met up with their relatives for the annual Tuttle Family Reunion. Ethan and Emily were excited for a week of fun with their cousins!

Mr. Tuttle set up the umbrellas for shade while the aunts and uncles talked about the traffic problem. They were all frustrated with how delayed they had been because of the closed road.

The twins were hungry. "Can we get some lunch now?" they asked their parents.

"C'mon you two, we were just about to pick up some food ourselves. Lunch is on me," Uncle Ben said.

"That's very kind of you, Ben," Mr. Tuttle replied.

The twins grabbed their scooters and went with Ben and his family to La Playa Lane.

At Kelly's Chowder House, Emily ordered fish and chips and Ethan got shrimp with fried clams covered in tartar sauce. "Ew, those clams are gross!" Emily told him, as Ethan grabbed another.

Some of their cousins got french fries, but they threw most of them at the hungry seagulls.

As they were eating, a couple of strangers walked up to Ben, shook his hand excitedly, and asked to take a photo with him.

"Who was that?" Ethan asked after they left.

"Oh, them?" Ben replied sheepishly. "Just some nice folks thanking me for doing my job."

"They thanked you for being a reporter?" Emily asked. "They were treating you like you're famous."

"Your uncle's videos are actually very popular on the Internet," Aunt Jasmine said with a wink.

After they finished eating, the twins rode down La Playa Lane to visit the other shops.

"Hey, what happened to Jack's Knick Knacks?" Ethan wondered out loud as they stopped in front of an abandoned building.

"And look over there," Emily pointed nearby. "The arcade and ice cream shop are closed, too!"

"Shutting down the old road is one thing," Ben told Ethan. "But now stores are closing their doors? I bet that these two things are connected. I smell a news story here..."

"Do you guys want to help me figure this out?" Ben asked the twins.

Ethan and Emily were both interested in getting to the bottom of this. They also thought it would be cool to help their uncle work on one of his videos.

Ben said he would try to figure out what happened to the old road. He then gave the twins a camera and a microphone and asked them to interview a shop owner to find out if they had any information about why the three businesses had recently closed.

The owner of the frozen banana stand told Ethan and Emily that the arcade, Jack's Knick Knacks, and the ice cream shop had moved to Surfdom, a beach further to the north.

"Why would they move away from La Playa Lane?" Emily asked.

"Well, Surfdom has become really popular lately—especially because the brand new road opened, and the one near our beach was closed. Many of the businesses from La Playa Lane are moving there into nice, new buildings," he said.

"Are you going to move your business, too?" Emily asked the shop owner.

"Me? Sadly, no," he replied, sighing. "I can't afford to move there. A lot of people want to use those new buildings, and that makes them worth a lot of money. Only bigger and more successful businesses can afford the cost. Surfdom is no place for a little shop like mine."

The shop owner dipped two frozen bananas in chocolate, rolled them in chopped peanuts and handed them to the twins. "My banana stand has usually helped me pay our family's bills, but if crowds at La Playa get too small, I may just have to shut it down."

15

Shortly after the interview, the twins arrived at the beach house just as Uncle Ben's car pulled up.

"Here are some old newspapers that I borrowed from the library," Ben said, dropping a stack on the hood of the car. "It looks like a few years ago, voters approved a Master Transportation Plan. It was started last year, and the government just completed it."

"But why would they build a new highway that would make it harder for us to get to La Playa?"

16

"That's the question of the day," Ben replied, shrugging his shoulders. "What did you guys learn from the folks at La Playa Lane?" he asked the twins.

Emily explained that the closed shops had moved to Surfdom. "I guess that's the cool beach everybody is going to now," she said.

Ben rubbed his chin as he thought. "I bet that new road goes straight to Surfdom. We need to talk to the residents in town. You guys want to come?"

After getting permission from their mom and dad, Ethan and Emily hopped in their uncle's car and drove to the neighborhood where all the traffic had been that morning.

"Do you notice all the For Sale signs?" Ben asked them. "We need to find out why everyone is trying to sell their home."

As they went door to door, Ben and the twins quickly learned what was going on: some people were upset that their streets were constantly full of cars. They didn't want to live there anymore.

The twins talked to one little girl in a cast who said she had been hit by a speeding car while riding her bike. Now she was scared to go near the street.

One older man said, "I supported the government's plan to build a new road further north so that there would be less traffic in town. But right now, traffic seems worse than usual."

They also came across some people who were loading up a moving truck.

"Excuse me, ma'am," Emily said. "May I ask why you're moving?"

"The creamery where I work is moving to another city far away. Many people in town are losing their jobs because of it," she replied. "I tried to sell my house, but with the creamery moving away, there won't be as many jobs around here. It seems that nobody wants to buy in this part of town."

"I'm really sad about that girl in the cast," Emily said on the drive back.

"Me, too," Ben said. "And that creamery has been in this town for a hundred years. Now I'm even more determined to figure out what's happening."

"I bet it has something to do with Surfdom," Ethan said. Ben agreed, and the group decided to drive there to investigate.

Uncle Ben and the twins headed toward Surfdom, driving on the newly built road.

"There are a lot of new houses over there," Emily said, pointing alongside the road to Surfdom. "Isn't this where that dairy farm used to be?"

Ethan remembered how they used to hold their noses whenever they were driving nearby because of the stinky smell from all the cows.

Ben pointed out the billboards announcing entire new neighborhoods opening up along the road.

As seagulls flew over their heads, Emily wondered what the view would be like from the sky. Probably just a bunch of rooftops, she imagined to herself.

As they arrived and headed toward the beach, the twins noticed a large walkway leading to a wide entrance, with a bright sign that could be seen from far away.

"Wow, Surfdom looks really nice..." Emily said as they walked in. She was staring wide-eyed at all the colorful shops and carnival rides. Ethan was recording some video footage with the camera.

"Hey, there's Jack's Knick Knacks!" said Ethan, pointing to the new shop. Emily noticed the arcade and ice cream shop were further down the way, and packed full of people.

Compared to La Playa, Surfdom was bigger, newer, and had a lot more people. Of course, it was easier for all those people to get there because of the new highway that had been built recently.

"We'd better get back," Ben said. "Grandma and Grandpa are playing the ukulele around the campfire tonight, plus I'm sure everyone will want to hear about this place."

The whole Tuttle family sat around a fire, singing and laughing as Grandma and Grandpa Tuttle performed some silly songs with their ukuleles.

Later, the twins told everybody about the road to Surfdom, the closing businesses, the creamery, and the homes that couldn't sell. It seemed everything was falling apart in the town near La Playa.

"Be careful what you wish for..." said Grandpa Tuttle to himself, but loudly enough for others to hear.

"What does that mean, Grandpa?" Ethan asked.

"Oh, it's an old saying," he replied. "Some of the people in town didn't like all the traffic, so they supported the government's plan to build a new road and change where everybody drives. Their wish has come true, but in ways that they didn't expect."

"Seeing all that newly developed land makes me think that it is also part of the story somehow," Ben remarked. "I think we may have found another piece of the puzzle."

The next morning, the whole Tuttle family decided that they would spend the day at Surfdom so they could see what it was like.

On the way there they drove through one of the newly built neighborhoods. It looked like many people had already moved in.

At the end of the street they came to the old farm house that had always been there, back when the entire area was still a dairy farm.

"One more interview," Uncle Ben told the twins.

"Good morning," said a man in a rocking chair on the front porch as they approached. "May I help you?"

Uncle Ben reached out and shook the man's hand. "My name is Ben, and this is my niece Emily and my nephew Ethan. We're hoping you might answer some questions about what happened to the old dairy farm that used to be here."

A look of deep sadness came across the man's face. "My name is Daniel Sanchez. Please come in."

"Please forgive the mess," he said. "It's taking so long to pack up this house. So many memories..." Boxes were stacked everywhere! When the twins asked why he was moving, Mr. Sanchez explained, "It doesn't feel like home to me anymore. The government stole my family's farm."

"What?! How can that happen?" Ethan asked in disbelief.

Mr. Sanchez began searching through some of the boxes as the twins eagerly waited for an answer.

"¡Aquí está!" he said to himself. He handed the twins a piece of paper that said EMINENT DOMAIN.

"This is what allowed the government to take the farm that had been in my family for five generations," Mr. Sanchez explained. From the wall he took a family photo that reminded the twins of their own family. "We tried everything we could to stop them," he replied. His eyes began filling with tears. "This is the only home we have ever known."

Mr. Sanchez explained how he resisted the government taking his land for months until finally some police officers arrived along with a construction crew that was ready to begin building the road right through the middle of the farm.

"The road made it impossible to graze my cattle here," he said. "Then some developers offered me a lot of money to sell the rest of my land to build this neighborhood. I didn't want to sell it, but by then I didn't have much of a choice; I couldn't use the land. So I took the money and lost the dairy farm forever."

"I think we have all the pieces for our story now," Ben remarked to the twins. "We're very sorry for what has happened, Mr. Sanchez. Thanks for sharing your story."

With the interview finished, the family's caravan continued down the road to Surfdom. It was a much nicer drive than the traffic they experienced at La Playa.

The outdoor games, the large fire pits, the awesome shops, and even the bathrooms were new and exciting at Surfdom. Everyone was impressed!

It was popular, too—the beach was packed with people. The road to Surfdom was bringing a lot of visitors to the newly constructed attractions.

The twins began building a sand castle, but they didn't seem too happy. "Don't you like it here?" Mrs. Tuttle asked her children.

"It's alright," Ethan said. "But it's hard to be excited about Surfdom when I can't stop thinking about the Sanchez family and all of the problems at La Playa."

"Mom, why did things have to change?" Ethan asked. "La Playa was really fun and popular and now everybody is going to Surfdom," he added.

Just then a wave came really close to the castle. "Oh no, the tide is coming in!" Emily yelled. They all began digging a moat to protect the castle.

"That's what happens with *central planning*—when a few people make decisions for everybody," said Mrs. Tuttle as she piled up buckets of sand to create a wall for extra protection.

"Some thought it would be a good idea to have the government build a new road," she continued. "But their plan has affected everybody else."

"Think about it," Mr. Tuttle said. "Why would anyone want to drive on a small, old road full of traffic to go to La Playa, when they can come to this amazing beach on a brand new road? The government's plans change people's actions. It even causes them to do things they wouldn't have otherwise done."

Another wave came crashing toward the castle, filling the moat and hitting Mrs. Tuttle's wall. The castle was protected—just as the family planned!

"Ugh, my towel is wet!" Emily shouted. The wall had channeled much of the water to the side, and while it protected the castle, the water was redirected to where the family's towels were.

"See what happened?" Mr. Tuttle asked his kids. "We made a mistake building this castle too close to the ocean. So we built the wall and moat to fix the problem, but that just caused different problems."

"Here's the lesson: even though central planning can help in some ways, it can also create problems."

"Central planning stinks!" groaned Emily, picking up her dripping towel.

"But aren't you always saying we should plan for the future?" Ethan asked. "Does that mean planning is bad?"

"It's great to plan for yourself," Mr. Tuttle replied. "When you're free to make your own plans, you can do what you think is best for you. You're also more careful to not make mistakes. Also, planning for yourself doesn't force other people to follow your plans. This is called *individualism*—when people are free to run their own lives as they wish."

Mrs. Tuttle pointed to the shops nearby. "Individuals didn't plan to move their businesses into these new shops on their own. The government's plan to put a new road in changed where people went—but look at all the harm it caused to the community around La Playa.

"When a few people make decisions they think will benefit the most people—and then force everybody to follow those decisions—that's called *collectivism*. It prevents individuals from making the best choices for themselves."

INDIVIDUALISM

COLLECTIVISM

"My plan is that we bury Ethan in a big hole in the sand!" Emily said with a giggle. When their parents sided with her, Ethan agreed to let them do it.

"Achoo!" sneezed Ethan because of some sand tickling his nose. "I'm not sure I like collectivism very much," he said.

"The government tries to plan how people should act—whether it's what beach they go to, or what their schools should teach, or what they can do with their property," Mr. Tuttle explained as he helped pull Ethan out of the sand. "But when people are free to make their own plans for themselves, everybody is happier and more prosperous."

"Hey Ethan, that's exactly what we learned at the pencil factory!" Emily said. The twins remembered the field trip where they had learned how millions of people work together to make lots of amazing things—without central planning.

Some of the extended family wanted to stay at a fancy new hotel at Surfdom that night, but the twins wanted to return to the beach house at La Playa.

Mrs. Tuttle explained during the car ride back that in some countries, the government plans so poorly that people can't buy milk, bread, gasoline, or even toilet paper.

"Ew, are you serious?" Emily asked. She had never imagined what her life would be like without any toilet paper!

"Sometimes, those in government seem to think that they are *omniscient*—that they know everything," her dad explained to the twins.

"But the people who work for the government are like you and me—we make mistakes, we don't know everything, and we can't predict the future. A few people can't really plan what millions of people should do. It never works!"

As the car neared La Playa Lane, the full moon shone brightly on the shops. "Oh no!" Ethan shouted. "The sign for the taco stand is gone. I wonder if they also had to close down..."

"Remember how our towels got wet today?" his father asked. "That was an accident. It's what we call an *unintended consequence*—something that happened but wasn't part of the original plan."

"I bet the government didn't plan for this to happen to La Playa," he added, "but it's definitely a consequence of what they've done by building the road to Surfdom and changing the traffic pattern."

"The sad thing is that so many of the people who have been hurt by the road to Surfdom once wanted it to be built. They definitely didn't expect all of this to happen!"

On their last night at the beach house, Ethan and Emily hopped into bed as they listened to the waves crash outside. They loved feeling the cool ocean breeze come through the window.

Just then, Mr. Tuttle's cell phone chimed. "Ben just sent me a link to his report," he said. They all snuggled close together to watch. Ethan and Emily were excited to see how Ben was going to share the story with the public!

"Tonight's Reality Check investigation is a story of central planning gone wrong," Ben told the viewers.

Ben continued: "How did one of the area's most popular beaches, La Playa, go from a community of prosperity to nearly a ghost town so quickly? You might be surprised to find out that the new road to Surfdom, which was planned to help the area's traffic problem, is in fact the very reason for the economic troubles the town now faces. My team and I investigated to find how it's all connected."

"When the government created the transportation plan, we supported it." Ethan and Emily grinned as they saw the man they had interviewed in the video. "But we didn't know it would affect us like this."

"If crowds at La Playa get too small, I may have to shut down," said the banana stand owner. Ben explained how businesses were moving to Surfdom.

Then Ben showed how the creamery had moved, causing many people to lose their jobs. "Nobody wants to buy my house, so I can't move along with the creamery," a woman said. "I lost my job!"

Mr. Sanchez told viewers how the road to Surfdom took much of his family's land, leading him to have to sell the rest. "The dairy farm is gone!" he said.

Ben explained how the new road caused the surrounding land to become very valuable to big businesses and home builders.

After the government took much of the Sanchez family's land and their dairy farm closed, this led the historic creamery to move elsewhere, causing many people to lose their jobs and abandon their homes and businesses at La Playa. The video showed the once-great boardwalk that now looked almost abandoned.

"So here's what you need to know," Ben concluded. "When it comes to central planning, be careful what you wish for, because you just might get it."

"Wow, Ben really knows how to break a story," Mrs. Tuttle said. "It all makes sense now."

Ethan and Emily planned to share Ben's video with all of their friends to help it go viral. They wanted others to learn about central planning and collectivism—without getting their towels wet or sand in their nose!

On their last day at the beach, some of the twins' cousins wanted to go back to Surfdom. Ethan and Emily didn't want to.

"Are you sure?" their mother asked them.

"I like this beach better," Ethan said. "And being at Surfdom just doesn't make me happy, especially because I know how it hurt a lot of people."

"Same here," Emily added. "And besides, now La Playa is less crowded, so there are more waves for me!" she said, racing Ethan to the water.

Mr. and Mrs. Tuttle agreed that sometimes it was best to take the road less traveled.

The End

Hi, parents! I'm F.A. Hayek, a Nobel Prize-winning, free-market economist.

There are several "schools of thought" when it comes to economics—differing beliefs as to what role, if any, the government should play in regulating the economy.

I'm part of the "Austrian school," which contends that market trends and social forces are the result of the combined actions and motivations of individuals—and that government policy should respect and protect people's decisions. In other words, that's what we call a free market.

I wrote *The Road to Serfdom* in the early 1940s to warn people "of the danger of tyranny that inevitably results from government control of economic decision-making through central planning." As I note in the book, the abandonment of individualism inevitably leads to a loss of freedom, the creation of an oppressive society, and the serfdom of the individual.

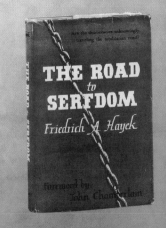

Sound familiar? It should. You're living through the very fulfillment of what I described.

The Author

Connor Boyack is president of Libertas Institute, a free market think tank in Utah. In that capacity he has changed a significant number of laws in favor of personal freedom and free markets, and has launched a variety of educational projects, including The Tuttle Twins children's book series. Connor is the author of over a dozen books.

A California native and Brigham Young University graduate, Connor currently resides in Lehi, Utah, with his wife and two children.

The Illustrator

Elijah Stanfield is owner of Red House Motion Imaging, a media production company in Washington.

A longtime student of Austrian economics, history, and the classical liberal philosophy, Elijah has dedicated much of his time and energy to promoting the ideas of free markets and individual liberty. Some of his more notable works include producing eight videos in support of Ron Paul's 2012 presidential candidacy. He currently resides in Richland, Washington, with his wife April and their six children.

Contact us at TuttleTwins.com!

Glossary of Terms

Central planning: Controlling the actions of individuals in order to manipulate an outcome; using the force of government to change people's behavior to meet a desired goal.

Collectivism: Forcing individuals to act in a way that others have decided to be the "common good" to allegedly benefit the most people; prioritizing a group of people over each individual in it.

Eminent domain: Taking a person's private property to be used for a purpose determined by the government to be more beneficial.

Individualism: Protecting the right of individuals to act in a way they decide is best for themselves; prioritizing the individual over the interests of any group he or she may be a part of.

Omniscience: Knowing everything.

Unintended consequence: The result of an action that is unanticipated. Central planning inevitably produces unforeseen results that harm people—something not intended by those in power, but a predictable byproduct of government planning nonetheless.

Discussion Questions

1. Why shouldn't a few people make decisions for the many?
2. How can unintended consequences be avoided?
3. Is central planning ever okay?
4. What are some current hot topics that demonstrate collectivism over individualism?

Don't Forget the Activity Workbook!

Visit **TuttleTwins.com/SurfdomWorkbook** to download the PDF and provide your children with all sorts of activities to reinforce the lessons they learned in the book!